TRUMP'S IGNORANCE IS NOT BLISS

BY
DR. MURRAY SIEGEL

DEDICATION

This book is dedicated to my wife, Sharon, who proofreads everything I write, and generally makes my words sound better.

INTRODUCTION

When scholars write the history of the United States during the second decade of the 21st century, one name will tower over all others, and that name is Donald J. Trump. There have been many columns already published by Trump-lovers and Trump-haters alike, with a full spectrum of opinions about the man and his politics.

This is a collection of one man's opinion, as written in columns from 2015 through 2019 in a weekly town newspaper. Many of the readers of that periodical were supporters of Trump, so the judgments could not be too sharp. They are in chronological order, from the race for the nomination, through the election and ending with the first two years of the Trump administration.

TABLE OF CONTENTS

Part One

THE RACE FOR THE NOMINATION

(September 2015-August 2016)

Part Two

THE ELECTION

(September 2016-December 2016)

Part Three

THE TRUMP ADMINISTRATION

(January 2016-January 2019)

PART ONE

The Race for the Nomination

(September 2015-July 2016)

One Man's Opinion

An Outsider as President?

Among the leading presidential candidates, four can be classified as outsiders — Dr. Ben Carson, Carly Fiorina, Senator Bernie Sanders, and Donald Trump. Voters who have grown weary of gridlock in Washington seek fresh faces and these four have tapped into this frustration. The question must be asked, can any of these candidates be a successful president? Except for Bernie Sanders, they have no experience getting laws passed through a Congress that can be stubborn even when the majority is of the same party as the president (see G.W. Bush and immigration). Jimmy Carter struggled because he did not understand how to get laws passed in DC. President Obama had limited experience in the U.S. Senate, and he has struggled to figure out how to get needed legislation passed. Do we need another president-in-training?

Dr. Carson is an extremely intelligent and articulate man. He was raised in a tough neighborhood in a single-parent family and rose to become a renowned brain surgeon. Even if you disagree with him on philosophy, you will listen because he seems so reasonable. Despite his intellect and rationality, how will he get legislation passed?

Ms. Fiorina has a "wonderful secretary-to-CEO" story. She is well-equipped to deal with business leaders and foreign leaders, but how will she get along with Congress? As CEO, she could fire a thousand people with the wave of her hand. Could she terminate even one Veterans' Administration failed bureaucrat without running into Civil Service laws?

Senator Sanders has a great deal of experience in Congress. He is listed as a liberal independent who caucuses with the Democrats. He is a self-declared socialist. As a socialist, he believes in single-payer healthcare and more federal expenditures. As a socialist, he must also believe that the government should own the means of production (GM, Apple, Microsoft, American Airlines, to name a few).

Mr. Trump is a larger-than-life personality, but could he get things done in DC? He can fire people in business and on television, but what will he do when faced with the rules of Civil Service? He can take a company to Chapter 11 bankruptcy and leave creditors in the cold. What can he legally do about the federal deficit and national debt? A president *actually has* limited powers and that could frustrate a President Trump to the point of acting irrationally.

We must assume that these four outsiders want to see our nation prosper. We must ask whether any of them is fit to be president in the environment in which the president must exist?

I leave it up to you to decide.

September 2015

One Man's Opinion

Why Is Trump Still Ahead?

Many observers find Donald Trump to be an egotistical bully and many political gurus have found misstatements and untruths in what he has uttered, yet potential Republican voters still favor him above all others. Why? Most Americans are angry and frustrated with our federal government's inability to get anything of importance done. Nothing on the economy, or immigration, or infrastructure or tax reform, or ....! Trump offers to make America great and to provide the leadership to help all Americans. He does not offer many specifics beyond his promises to get things done. He says he is not a politician, yet when he makes his empty promises, he is performing as many politicians have.

In 1916, Woodrow Wilson was re-elected president because he kept us out of the war. A month after his inauguration, we declared war on Germany. FDR was re-elected in 1940 because he kept our nation out of the European war, and we know what happened in 1941. In 1964, LBJ stated that he would not send American boys to do what Vietnamese boys should be doing. How come, four years later, I, an American boy, was dropping bombs on North and South Vietnam? In 1968, Nixon had a secret means of ending the Vietnam War, yet four years later, Americans were still dying over there. In 2008, Barack Obama promised to end gridlock and bring hope and change to our nation. How has that worked?

Trump is not the only candidate who is making promises without specifics. Carly Fiorina would bring back the Sixth Fleet but does not tell us how we will pay for it. Senator Ted Cruz promises to tear up the nuclear agreement with Iran but does not explain what good that will do if the rest of the world honors the pact and trades with Iran. They are all politicians, it is just that Trump's promises are the most vacuous and are not backed up with any specifics.

No matter which presidential candidate you favor, please investigate his/her promises before you vote.

September 2015

One Man's Opinion

Restricting Immigration

Presidential contender Donald Trump has declared that Muslims should be denied entry into our country and a significant percentage of Republican voters seem to support that point of view. According to surveys, the folks who back the no-Muslim philosophy tend to be from rural areas and generally have no more than a high school diploma. The meaning of these demographics will be left to you.

Of greater interest is the question, "Is Trump falling back on an American tradition?" There was a political party that was opposed to the entry into our nation of foreigners whose religion was different than theirs. These Americans feared that members of this foreign religion were influenced by the leadership of their faith who were hostile to American ideals. The primary goal of these politicians was to limit the entry into the U.S. of unwanted foreigners.

Who were the philosophical ancestors of Donald Trump? Originally their party was named the Native American Party but that was quickly changed to simply the American Party. The immigrants they sought to keep away from our shores were Germans and Irish. The religion they sought to keep out of America was Roman Catholicism, and the foreign religious leader they feared was the Pope. This was back in the 1850s and the American Party was also known as the Know-Nothings. This name was derived from the response party members gave when asked about the party. They claimed to know nothing. What would Trump and his supporters say when asked to justify their no-Muslim policy in terms of law, morality, and the American way?

The influence of the Know-Nothings waned quickly, and their efforts were totally extinguished by William McKinley, Republican candidate for the presidency in 1896. McKinley courted the Catholic vote and won a major victory. It is said by political pundits that McKinley, acting on the belief that those who were not White Protestants were as much American as anyone else, led to a sea change in American Presidential politics.

Trump, his advisers, and his staunch supporters should read about the Know-Nothings and President William McKinley.

December 2015

One Man's Opinion

Vote for Trump/Cruz and Elect Hillary!

Many conservative Republicans are absolutely fed up with our Federal Government. They have no use for President Obama, who they feel is leading our nation down the wrong path. They are also angry with establishment Republicans in Congress, who were elected to counter the president and have done little to keep their promises. Some of the angry Republicans are supporting Donald Trump, despite his less-than-conservative roots and his outrageous statements. An increasing number of conservative Republicans are moving towards Senator Ted Cruz. If either of these candidates is the Republican nominee for president, you can count on Secretary Hillary Clinton being our next president.

I do not support Hillary, but one must take a realistic look at the electoral college since it is this body that determines who is elected president — NOT the popular vote. When you see national polls, you should disregard them unless they consider the electoral votes of each state. There are blue states that would give their electoral votes to any Democrat and there are red states who will vote Republican no matter who the candidate is. You should note that blue states are smaller in size than the red states, but they have greater populations and thus, a larger number of electoral votes.

The only way for a Republican to be elected president is to win most, if not all, the swing (or battleground) states, such as Ohio, Florida, and North Carolina. The citizens who make the difference in the swing states are the independent voters, and independents tend to be more moderate than hardcore Republicans or Democrats. Will independents vote for Trump or Cruz? Remember that independents tend to have a higher than average level of education and many independents are Hispanic. Trump makes proclamations that independents find ridiculous. Cruz appears to be more interested in following the dictates of his political beliefs rather than accomplishing what our nation needs. Read the writings of Hamilton, Jay, and Madison when they explained the U.S. Constitution and you will realize the importance of compromise. Our government is based on compromise, yet Ted Cruz finds compromise unconscionable.

Hillary Clinton may be the weakest Democratic presidential candidate since Michael Dukakis, but a majority of independents will vote for her if the other choice is Cruz or Trump.

So, if you are a supporter of either of those candidates, look at the electoral map, think about who the independent voters are, and find a Republican candidate who can win the electoral college vote.

December 2015

One Man's Opinion

A Great Businessman?

Donald Trump has a large group of passionate supporters who continue to stand for the man, despite his bullying behavior, despite his obvious ignorance about national security, diplomacy, and military weapons, and despite his saying something then denying he ever said it. Why such loyalty? If you ask the folks in the Trump crowd, they will tell you that he is a great businessman and we need somebody who can successfully run a business to run our country. They know that he has been a successful entrepreneur and the supporters will trumpet his phenomenal wealth, however, his wealth and his business acumen need to be examined closely.

An article in *Forbes* magazine looked at three billionaires and the growth in their net worth from 1988 until today. Donald Trump went from one billion to four billion dollars. Warren Buffett, in that same interval, went from 2.5 billion to sixty-eight billion and Bill Gates grew his fortune from one billion to eighty billion. How successful was Trump?

What deserves closer investigation are some of Trump's business failures. Trump Airlines was purchased in 1988. He converted it from a no-frills shuttle service to a luxury airline. He defaulted on bank loans and creditors took over the airline, which folded in 1992. Trump Vodka was rolled out in 2006 and stopped production in 2011, due to lack of interest. The three Trump Casinos, all located in Atlantic City, declared bankruptcy for the **fourth** time in 2014. Trump claimed no connection to the casinos other than his name, but he owned twenty-eight percent of the company stock. *Trump* Magazine began publishing in 2007 and stopped production a year and a half later. Trump Steakhouse, located in Las Vegas, closed in 2010 after receiving fifty-one health code violations. Trump Mortgage remained in business for less than two years. Trump University opened in 2007, and in 2010, students sued the university saying that classes were no more than infomercials. Eventually the New York Attorney General sued Trump University for allegedly defrauding students.

These are the results of Trump's business acumen — failures and bankruptcies, with investors, students, and taxpayers taking the losses. Is this the man we want running our country? If you still say, "Yes", then you may need to take a class on comprehending facts and making a rational approach to decision making.

Good luck!

March 2016

One Man's Opinion
Who is Gary Johnson?

Many voters, especially those who claim to be independent, have a serious dilemma as they consider their vote in the November presidential election. Many will not vote for Donald Trump, who they do not see as a serious candidate. Although many of these voters respect the experience and intelligence of Hillary Clinton, they cannot abide her lack of integrity or moral character. So, who gets their vote? Perhaps they should consider Gary Johnson, the likely presidential candidate of the Libertarian Party.

Gary Johnson was a two-term Republican governor of New Mexico (1995 to 2003) and ran for president on the Libertarian ticket in 2012. If you have an opportunity to hear him speak, you will find that he is a rational man with strong convictions. You may find that you agree with many of his stances on important questions, but you will also find strong disagreement with other positions he takes.

He is a devoted fiscal conservative who believes in smaller government. His platform includes reducing the national debt without raising taxes, simplifying the tax code and accelerating job growth by eliminating unnecessary regulations. He would use the military only to keep Americans safe and sees ISIS as our primary threat. He believes that education is not a federal responsibility and favors school choice.

Gary Johnson is also a social liberal. He believes that the government should not tell adults how to act if their actions do no harm to others. He supports the legalization of marijuana and same-sex marriage. As long as abortion is legal, he says that the government should not interfere with a woman's right to choose, although, as governor, he supported a ban on late-term abortions.

His stance on immigration is based on a belief that a work visa program, along with an uncompromising employment ID verification system, will eliminate illegal entry. He has said that building a taller wall will only lead to the construction of longer ladders. He strongly favors criminal justice reform, including allowing those who have served their time and completed all post-release requirements to vote. He questions the validity of NSA collection of communication data.

If enough voters decide that Gary Johnson would be a better president than Donald or Hillary, perhaps he can actually garner some electoral college votes and that might cause the election to be decided by the House of Representatives for the first time since 1876.

Wouldn't it be a wonderful civics lesson?

May 2016

One Man's Opinion

Who Took All Those Jobs?

Among the supporters of Bernie Sanders and Donald Trump, there are numerous Americans who believe that the American Dream of a middle-class life has been destroyed by greedy capitalists and foreign governments, abetted by recent American presidents and Congresses. Are these accusations accurate? In 1971, sixty-one percent of Americans were in the middle class while today, about one-half of our citizens are middle-class. Many of those who fell out of the middle-class status are persons whose education stopped with high school.

It is true that in 1960, twenty-eight percent of U.S. jobs were in manufacturing while today, that number is less than nine percent. Did all those jobs go to Mexico and Asia? Actually, the move of plants overseas started well before the Clinton administration. Corporations could not make a reasonable profit given the labor costs. These companies made two adjustments. One was to move their plants overseas where the reduced cost of manpower more than compensated for the cost of shipping the goods to our shores. They also built new plants in the U.S which incorporated modern technology, reducing the size of the labor force and contributing to increased productivity. There are high-paying manufacturing jobs available here today, but the applicant needs to have a background in computers, robotics or statistical process control. Those angry voters who want a better paying job need to go back to school, get the necessary training and find the type of work that will put them back into the middle-class.

What can Trump or Sanders do to bring jobs back to America? How about imposing high tariffs on imported goods? That might destroy overseas competition, but it would mean that $25 shirt made in Vietnam would now cost $45.

How about those good white-collar jobs that existed a generation ago? Here, too, technology was used to reduce the labor force. When you make an airline reservation or switch funds from checking to savings, you probably do it online without any interaction with a human. And, if you should call customer service, you will speak with a human who resides in South Asia. Will Sanders or Trump make using technology illegal?

To see a solution, take a close look at South Carolina. This small state has major manufacturing facilities from more than twenty countries within the state's borders— companies such as BMW, Fuji Film, Michelin and Honda. This was accomplished by the state creating a network of technical schools where citizens could receive state-of-the-art training leading to good, financially rewarding jobs.

Stop blaming business or government and get the training you need to secure your future!

May 2016

One Man's Opinion

The Return of Manufacturing Jobs

I recently heard Donald Trump make a presentation on his plan to improve the American economy. He promised that when he is president, manufacturing plants will return to the U.S. and many new high-paying jobs will allow Americans to return to middle-class status. He derided trade treaties such as NAFTA for taking jobs from American workers. He blamed President Bill Clinton for NAFTA and its aftermath. He further promised to cancel all these trade deals and renegotiate better ones. As usual, he spoke with a fervor that causes his supporters to rise to their feet and cheer. The question remains if what he says is true.

There is no question that NAFTA brought pain to certain U.S. industries, but other areas of our economy were positively affected by it. Furthermore, manufacturing plants were being moved to Mexico and Asia **well before** NAFTA was signed. Labor costs were simply much cheaper overseas and the savings on labor more than compensated for the cost of transporting the manufactured goods to our shores. Those high wages and great benefits experienced by American manufacturing workers priced their products out of the market. It should be noted that although NAFTA was finalized during the Clinton administration, the foundation work on NAFTA was accomplished under President George H.W. Bush.

How will a President Trump accomplish the revitalization of American manufacturing and overcome the price advantage possessed by overseas manufacturers due to lower labor costs? Let's take a simple example. Currently you can buy a nice shirt, made in Vietnam, for $35. If that item was made in America and the workers were paid those middle-class salaries, the shirt might cost $60. Will you pay the extra $25 for the same shirt because it was American-made? Probably not, so the Trump administration would place a $25 tariff on these imported shirts, allowing American shirts to be competitive since the American shirt would cost $60 as would the imported ones (35 + 25 = 60). Of course, by paying more for items due to tariffs, your newly increased income will be chewed up by significantly higher prices. In addition, foreign countries upset with American tariffs on their exports will place their own tariffs on American imports to their country, thus reducing the profitability of American industries that derive much of their profits from exports.

If "President" Trump has a different plan, we need to hear its specifics. Otherwise, we must believe that his economic plan is no more honest than his statement about Muslims in New Jersey celebrating the destruction of 9/11, which turned out to be a fabrication.

June 2016

One Man's Opinion

Promises and Consequences

When a politician is running for office, it is highly likely that he or she will make promises about all the wonderful things that will happen if he or she is elected. Rarely do these promises include an explanation of the source of the funding needed to meet the promise and never do these promises include a detailing of possible negative consequences. In 1968, Richard Nixon promised to end the war in Vietnam, which he did, but it took four years and cost 20,000 American lives. Forty years later Barack Obama promised Hope and Change. How has that worked out? The current competition for president is a perfect example of this. Recently, I watched presentations by both major party candidates, and each made a promise that deserves further investigation.

Hillary Clinton promised that if she is elected president, there will be free community college and debt-free four-year college educations. That sounds good if you have children or grandchildren approaching college-age, but no explanation is made of how she will pay for this wonderful benefit. Colleges, both two-year and four-year, rely on tuition for a major source of revenue. What will replace this lost revenue? We can raise taxes! Another option would be to simply add the cost to the national debt, which does not immediately affect most people until the debt gets out of hand – our national debt is closing in on twenty trillion dollars and many would say that this amount is getting out of hand. A third option is to reduce federal expenditures. We can do away with the CDC, the FAA, and the Federal Highway Administration, and stop federal inspection of meat and drugs. Does that sound advisable to you? We do not know how Secretary Clinton plans to pay for her promise. As for possible consequences of it, colleges could save vast amounts of money by increasing class size — instead of ten instructors teaching English 101 in classes of thirty students, we could have one instructor teaching the class with 300, but that would not promote effective learning.

Meanwhile, Donald Trump promised that if the Carrier Corporation builds air conditioners in Mexico and tries to sell them in the U.S., as president, he would add a 35% tax — actually, a tariff. Sounds like a plan to prevent American companies from moving plants overseas, but wait, will we now be paying more for air conditioners? What if Mexico places a tariff on American exports? That will reduce our exports and possibly cost American jobs. Tariffs generally do not work and lead to trade wars, which are disastrous for all nations.

The next time Hillary or Donald makes a promise, demand to know the consequences of it!

July 2016

PART TWO

The

Election

(September 2016-December 2016)

One Man's Opinion

"One Nation Under ONE God"

On a number of occasions, Donald Trump has declared that his goal when he is president is to have the U.S. be "one nation, under one God". You might say, "What's the big deal?" We say, "under God" during the Pledge of Allegiance and our currency states that "in God we Trust". There is a significant difference between "under God" and "under *one* God". Without the word "one", it is left up to the individual American to decide which God he or she believes we trust. A Buddhist or an atheist may perceive God as nature or the Cosmos. If we must pledge to one God, whose God is it? The LDS Church has a different perception of God than the Catholic Church. Is our one God the Islamic Allah, or perhaps, the Jewish Adonai? Maybe it is Zeus from ancient Greek mythology, or it could be Manitou, the god of many Native American peoples.

No matter which God President Trump would choose, he would be violating our Constitution, which proclaims that there is NO state religion and, thus, no one accepted God, while rejecting all others. Catholics came to Maryland, Quakers came to Pennsylvania, and Puritans came to Massachusetts to escape a state-determined religion. Separation of church and state is a fundamental foundation of our republic. Obviously, in 1789, the vast majority of Americans were Protestant. Since then, 227 years of immigration has brought Catholics, Jews, Muslims, Hindus, Buddhists, Shintos, Zoroastrians, and even more faiths to our shores.

Remember that many of our founding fathers were deists, who believed that there was a Creator and that He was mostly disinterested in human endeavors. We were free to make our own way through life.

Perhaps Mr. Trump should leave God to personal beliefs and houses of worship. Then he could focus on topics of great import to the success of our country – immigration, infrastructure, national debt, Social Security, Medicare, tax simplification and fairness, and upgrading educational opportunities so that folks can develop skills that will move them permanently into the middle class.

We should pray to the God in which we believe that he will do this. Amen!

September 2016

One Man's Opinion

The Vote for President

Many Americans are facing a difficult decision as they look forward to the election of the next president of the United States since they cannot support either candidate. This article is personal, and I will use the first person, which is something I usually try to avoid in my writing.

I am a registered Republican who has split his ticket over the years but has generally voted for more Republicans. I have voted in every presidential election since 1964 and most often have voted for the Republican nominee — I must admit that I voted against Richard Nixon in 1968 and 1972. This year, I cannot vote for Donald Trump. Despite his supporters denying it, Trump is an egotistical, thin-skinned demagogue, who has tapped into the vein of what is disturbing many Americans. However, I cannot believe that he is capable of solving their problems. His business successes have been in

Manhattan real estate and he has done some wonderful projects that helped New York. Most of the rest of his businesses have failed, leaving a trail of unpaid bills, lawsuits, and creditors holding worthless paper. He says something outrageous then says he did not say it then states that he was misunderstood. If this happened occasionally, one could forgive him. But whether it was when he talked about stopping Muslim admission to the U.S., Megan Kelly, Carly Fiorina, a "Mexican" judge, or the mother of a Muslim American soldier killed in combat saving his troops, Trump has consistently backpedaled.

On the other hand, I will not vote for Hillary Clinton. Her political career has consistently demonstrated a lack of integrity. She speaks as an attorney, which she is, twisting the meaning of words to meet her objectives — does she remind you of the question about what "is" is? If she appeared on television today and admitted to lying about e-mails, Libya, etc., that might please some critics, but I would have to ask, "Is she telling the truth now?" Her supporters claim that she is the best-prepared person to be president and they are correct. The caveat is that the last presidential nominee who was the best prepared to be president was Richard Nixon. His similar lack of integrity caused him to be the only president to ever resign in over two hundred years of administrations.

So, for whom shall I vote? I plan to vote for Gary Johnson, the Libertarian candidate. I do not agree with a number of his positions, yet I find him to be an intelligent and rational man. He was a successful two-term Republican governor in a blue state. You may say that by voting for him, I am helping to elect Hillary or Donald (your choice.)

I disagree and believe exactly what Ted Cruz said about voting your conscience.

When the last hanging chad is counted, putting either Clinton or Trump into the White House, and things get worse, I will be able to say that it is NOT my fault!

September 2016

One Man's Opinion

The Wall

Political pundits continue to claim that no matter how often Donald Trump changes his stance on a topic, as long as he sticks to talking about building the wall, his supporters will continue to endorse him. Unfortunately, there are four major problems with the Trump Wall. First, a wall across the entire U.S.-Mexico border will be outrageously expensive, with estimates running beyond one hundred billion dollars, and Mexico will NOT pay for it!

A second problem is that this wall is totally impractical. Much of the border is comprised of the Rio Grande. Building a wall in the river is extremely complicated and will present environmental challenges. Building it on the Mexican side is an act of war. If it is built on the American side, Mexico will totally control the Rio Grande. A third problem is that forty percent of undocumented aliens have entered the U.S. legally, but their student or tourist visas have expired. A wall would not halt this.

A fourth problem is that criminals, terrorists, and drug runners will not be stopped by a wall. They can simply enter the U.S. by traveling via boat to an isolated location on any of the vast stretches of American coastland.

It must be stated that during his speech, Mr. Trump mentioned three efforts that he will initiate as president which will have a powerful impact on reducing illegal entry. Vastly increasing the number of Border Patrol agents. Ensuring that they are on the border and not behind a desk would get trained agents where they need to be. He also indicated that he would vastly improve the E-Verify program, which forces employers to verify that employees are in this country legally. This would have to include checking on employers who hire day laborers. Finally, Mr. Trump mentioned that tracking down those who have overstayed their visas would be a high priority in his administration. If this form of illegal residence can be countered, it would mean reducing the undocumented population by almost one half.

These three programs are much more efficient than a wall, but there is one question. How will we pay for them? A major increase in the Border Patrol, upgrading of the E-Verify system and the investigations to ensure that all employers are complying, and a concentrated effort to root out those who have expired visas will all increase federal expenditures. Eighty-two percent of the federal budget covers Social Security, Medicare, the military, and interest on the national debt, so the funds for these effective tools would have to come from increasing the debt or raising taxes. These tools must be implemented immediately, which means the funds must be immediately available.

More taxes or more debt – which one would President Trump choose?

September 2016

One Man's Opinion

Questions That Must Be Asked

Throughout this election campaign, questions have been asked of the candidates. A few have been answered while most have been deflected. There are a few questions which have NOT been asked and it is important that somebody ask them and demand answers.

Hillary Clinton said that many of Trump supporters were deplorable and could not be redeemed. The question not asked is, "If Mrs. Clinton is a Methodist, how can she claim that there are folks who cannot be redeemed?" Redemption is a basic tenet of the Christian faith. Donald Trump finally admitted that President Obama was born in the U.S. The unasked question is, "What difference does it make where he was born?" Since his mother was an American citizen, he was born an American citizen. Please note that Ted Cruz was born in Calgary, Alberta, Canada, and John McCain was born in Coco Solo, Panama, and they were both U.S. citizens by birth since their mothers were Americans.

When folks argue against voter ID laws, they claim that there has been no evidence of voter fraud. The question is, "If there are no voter ID requirements, how do we know that there has not been significant voter fraud?"

Most rational citizens recognize that climate change is a fact, but what is in question is whether that change is due to human activity or simply a natural cycle of the Earth. The question that should be asked is, "Even if climate change is a natural occurrence, is it wise to release tons of carbon dioxide into the atmosphere? Will that exacerbate climate change?" Should a diabetic whose condition is due to genetics eat lots of sugar and carbohydrates because the diabetes was not his fault?

Some people blame Bill Clinton for NAFTA and they blame NAFTA for the loss of American jobs. The question to be asked is, "Is it not true that NAFTA negotiations were initiated by President George H.W. Bush and is it also not true that American manufacturing jobs began to move overseas well before NAFTA was ratified?" Some day in the future, while we are still around to see it, there will be a debate or press conference where a politician will be asked important questions and answers to those questions will be demanded!

Do not expect it this year.

October 2016

One Man's Opinion
Fake News vs. Real News

Recently fake news almost caused a real tragedy. A story was spread on social media that a pizza joint in DC was harboring a child-sex ring led by Hillary Clinton. Articles were published in the mainstream media showing that this story was totally untrue. After these articles went public, there was a post on Twitter from Representative Steve Smith from the Georgia 15th district, which warned that the information debunking the pizza/child-sex story itself was false. Smith's tweet was retweeted many times. There is no Georgia representative named Steve Smith and there is no 15th district in that state. A man in North Carolina read the "Pizzagate" stories and decided to rescue the children. He drove to Washington and entered the restaurant armed with a rifle and handgun. He fired the rifle but put down his weapons when he saw that there were no sex slaves there. Meanwhile, he thoroughly scared families that were eating there.

Fake news is not a new phenomenon. Forty years ago, customers waiting on the check-out line at the grocery store could see newspaper headlines announcing, "Hollywood Starlet Gives Birth to a Three-headed Baby" or "Aliens Take Over the State Legislature". Publications from extremist organizations would publish outrageous stories and a member of Congress would read the story into the Congressional Record. Mainstream media would then quote the Record, making the fake story legitimate. What is new today is the use of social media and cable outlets to spread unfounded stories. Also, many citizens do not trust the mainstream media. These media may filter news stories and give strong opinions in one direction or another, but news is supposed to be facts. What checks are there on social media, cable news organizations, or, for that matter, mainstream media, to prevent news from being published with zero factual basis?

A liberal activist tweets that President-elect Trump is an anti-Semite. Does anybody check to see that this is untrue? Trump's daughter and son-in-law, both important advisers, are Jewish (him by birth and her by choice.) Trump's grandchildren are Jewish, so how could he be hateful towards Jewish people? A conservative activist tweets that Chuck Schumer (minority leader of the Senate) was a member of a Communist club when he was in high school. Who takes the time to verify if this is true? Chuck was too busy being an honors student at Madison High School to join a communist organization, if there had even been one at that school. Something must be done to overcome fake news.

The citizens must demand truth in news and those who spread fake news must be punished!

December 2016

PART THREE

The
Trump
Administration

(January 2016-January 2019)

One Man's Opinion

A Legitimate President

A significant number of Americans, including some Democratic politicians, believe that Donald Trump is not a legitimate president. They claim that embarrassing e-mails released by WikiLeaks, which they received due to Russian hacking, as well as statements by the FBI Director, negatively affected the voting for Hillary Clinton and, thus, allowed Trump to be elected. Several presidential campaigns in recent history have been influenced by factors other than the candidate or the party platform.

In 1960, votes for JFK were recorded in Chicago for residents of a graveyard. In 1964, the Daisy ad convinced some voters that a vote for Goldwater would lead to nuclear war. President Ford's pardon of Richard Nixon reduced his chance to be elected in 1976. The Willie Horton ad of 1988 convinced voters that Michael Dukakis was soft on crime and his initial lead disappeared. The entry of H. Ross Perot as an independent candidate in 1992 paved the way for Clinton's defeat of Bush 41. A few thousand seniors in Palm Beach, FL, refused to ask for help in order to read the butterfly ballot. They thought they voted for Gore but actually voted for Pat Buchanan. If they had voted correctly, Al Gore would have been the forty-third president. The Swiftboaters challenged John Kerry's status as a war hero, which helped Bush 43 to be re-elected in 2004.

Did the WikiLeaks actions or the FBI Director's statements really cause the Trump victory? Clinton would have won Connecticut and California no matter what. Trump would have won South Carolina and Wyoming without any outside influences. What cost Clinton the election were rural and blue-collar voters in Michigan, Wisconsin and Pennsylvania casting their votes for Trump. These were people who had generally voted for Obama in 2008 and 2012. They did not pay attention to the FBI or WikiLeaks. They saw Clinton as dismissive of their problems and Trump as a candidate who listened and was prepared to help them.

Whether you think he is a savior or a self-serving demagogue, Donald Trump is the legitimate president. Stop wasting time in protests and be prepared to support the president when you agree with him and protest when he takes actions which you find objectionable. Those members of Congress who boycotted the inauguration were not protesting Trump, they were protesting the U.S. Constitution. As Americans, we should be exceedingly proud of the peaceful transition of power, despite the onerous campaign. Juxtapose that with the transition in the African county of Gambia. The president who had served twenty-two years was defeated in a landslide but refused to give up his presidency. Only the possible military intervention by neighboring countries convinced him to leave his office.

Whether you love Trump or fear him, we all should be delighted to be Americans.

January 2017

One Man's Opinion

Elections Have Consequences

In January 2009, recently-inaugurated President Obama met with Republican and Democratic leaders of the House and Senate. He was asked a question by either Senator John McCain or House Minority Whip Eric Cantor and the president's reply was alleged to have been that *elections have consequences*. In other words, the elected president makes the rules and the defeated minority party must suffer the consequences of failing in the election. What President Obama said is true and Democrats in the Senate should pay heed to that message.

Donald Trump is our president and he has the right to select whom he wants to become his cabinet secretaries and federal judges, including Supreme Court justices. There is no question that Republicans objected to some of Obama's selections for his cabinet and the

Supreme Court, just as Democrats now raise objections to Trump's nominees. Political disagreement is not a valid reason to hold up a president's nominee. You can vote against the nominee, but it is counterproductive for our country's success to delay the vote. If there is evidence of a crime committed by a nominee or some proof of corruption, provide the evidence. Otherwise, state your opposition but do not say that the nominee is unfit for his or her position.

Certainly, Republican senators objected to Eric Holder, who was Obama's first attorney general, or to Justice Elena Kagan, just as Democratic senators currently object to Jeff Sessions and Neil Gorsuch for the same positions. Jeff Sessions was challenged because of accusations made in 1986 of racial insensitivity. That was thirty years ago, and he was a white politician in Alabama. Did he commit a crime? If not, Trump has the right to have the attorney general he desires. Democrats will proclaim that Gorsuch is too conservative. They must remember that some folks voted for Trump for just one reason — he would appoint a conservative justice to take the seat of Antonin Scalia. That is exactly what he is doing.

Once a cabinet secretary or federal judge is sworn in, what can be done if he or she commits a crime or is corrupted? The answer is impeachment and there have been several judges and one cabinet secretary who were impeached. In 1876, Grant's secretary of war, William Belknap, was impeached for graft and corruption. Once he resigned, he was acquitted. In 1804, Supreme Court Associate Justice Samuel Chase was impeached for political bias in his rulings. He was acquitted. So, action can be taken.

Democrats should take heed now and Republicans should be prepared for when a Democrat wins the presidency.

Elections have consequences!

February 2017

One Man's Opinion

Confirm Judge Gorsuch Now

Your mother told you when you were a child that two wrongs do not make a right. Unfortunately, many Democrats in the U.S. Senate do not recall that motherly message. They are trying to hold up the ultimate confirmation of Judge Neil Gorsuch as an associate justice on the U.S. Supreme Court and their reasons are nonsense. They are angry that Merrick Garland, President Obama's nominee for the seat of Antonin Scalia, was never considered by the Republican Senate. Again, two wrongs do not make a right!

Democratic senators state that Gorsuch is out of the mainstream and that he tends to favor corporations over the "little man". He is a conservative judge, well within the mainstream of conservative judicial philosophy. Not one senator has charged Judge Gorsuch's opinions as being wrong based on the law. If a law is written to favor business over the worker, it is not biased if a judge decides in favor of the business because that is the law. Neil Gorsuch was appointed to his current position on the U.S. Court of Appeals, 10th Circuit, by President George W. Bush and was confirmed by a voice vote of the Senate, indicating no strong opposition to that appointment. Has he changed since then or is it simply politics holding up confirmation to the position that he will eventually obtain?

Yes, he is a conservative, but he would be replacing Justice Scalia, who was a conservative. Democrats should save their energy for a time when a liberal justice, such as Ruth Bader Ginsburg, must be replaced. If that appointment is made by a Republican, the balance of the court will be changed. If Democratic senators are so concerned about the make-up of the Supreme Court, they should have worked harder for Hillary Clinton in the 2016 presidential election.

If (or rather, when) Neil Gorsuch is confirmed, he will be the youngest appointee since Clarence Thomas, and he will be the only Protestant on the high court. All the current justices are either Catholic or Jewish. If a Democrat needs a reason to vote "yes" on Gorsuch, a good rationale would be that Gorsuch was a classmate of Barack Obama at Harvard Law School, so he cannot be all bad.

Confirm Neil Gorsuch and get back to the important business of the federal government.

March 2017

One Man's Opinion

Leaking vs. Unmasking

There have been accusations among supporters of President Trump about leaks of classified information by intelligence or security personnel in the Obama administration.

In explaining their concerns, the accusers have used the terms "leaking" and "unmasking" interchangeably, so that many citizens would assume that the terms are synonyms. The accusers have pointed out that leaking of classified information is a serious crime and they want to see the leakers identified, investigated, and punished. Indeed, the revealing of classified information by a person with the proper clearance to another person without the proper clearance is a crime.

Let us examine a hypothetical scenario. Person A is a high-level intelligence operative in the federal government. While looking over some documents describing a conversation between a Russian government official and an American, that was legally obtained, A sees that the American's name has been masked; that is the name is blacked out and cannot be seen. A has a need to know the identity of this person and applies to her superior for approval to unmask this name. If approved, the unmasking allows A, and only A, to see the name, which is identified here as B. B is a member of the new president's transition team or has been nominated by the president-elect to an important advisory position. When asked if he has had contact with Russian government officials, B firmly states that he has not. A knows that B is lying, and she reveals this information to a journalist or a politician, neither of whom have the proper clearance.

It must be noted that the unmasking is NOT a crime since it was done with proper security clearance and with approval by the appropriate superior. The leaking may be a crime. You may ask, "Why 'may be'"? Let's say somebody shoots another person with a gun. Is that a crime? The answer is that it depends on the circumstances. If the person who was shot had entered the shooter's home and was a threat, then it is justifiable and not a crime. So, if A was concerned about B's lies and the effect he might have on the new administration, she might see no choice but to reveal the truth so that it becomes public. Given this circumstance, it should be up to the FBI whether A committed a crime.

When you hear that a member of the Obama administration unmasked a Trump appointee, remember that this is not a crime. If the unmasking leads to a leak, then further investigation is needed.

Do not be fooled by an accuser using the term "unmasking" as if it were the same "leaking"!

April 2017

One Man's Opinion

Are You Surprised?

Many Americans are dismayed at the actions taken by President Donald Trump since his inauguration. The vast majority of Trump supporters are still with him and tend to blame the media for embellishing (perhaps untruthfully) his actions. No matter your position on his behavior, are you surprised? This column is written in the first person since I will quote from my columns written over the past two years in the *Monitor*, to demonstrate why I am not surprised in the least.

I did not vote for the president nor did I vote for Hillary Clinton. I believe that the president was legitimately elected. The FBI and the Russians did not cause Donald Trump to win the election. Clinton made the contest about Trump instead of about what she would do to get our nation back on track, and that was the reason she lost. President Trump has taken actions that I support. Justice Gorsuch was an outstanding choice for the Supreme Court. Responding militarily to Syria's use of chemical weapons was the right thing to do and dropping that huge bomb in Afghanistan made sense. His choices of Tillerson, Kelly, Mattis, Pompeo, and McMaster were top drawer. Unfortunately, some of his selections for domestic cabinet positions lack the same wisdom. He needs a chief of staff who is a Howard Baker clone, to protect the president from bad advice and from his own words. Reince Priebus is not that clone.

What about the president's apparent ignorance about running a government or about security procedures? In March 2016, I wrote, "Donald Trump has a large group of passionate supporters who continue to stand for the man despite his bullying behavior, **despite his obvious ignorance about national security, diplomacy, and military weapons**, and despite his saying one thing then denying he ever said it". How about his inability to get legislation for major programs accomplished, such as repealing/replacing Obamacare and instituting a travel ban? In September 2015, I wrote, "Mr. Trump is a larger-than-life personality, but could he get things done in DC? He can take a company to Chapter 11 bankruptcy and leave creditors in the cold. What can he legally do about the federal deficit and national debt? A president has limited powers and **that could frustrate a President Trump to act irrationally**".

In my September 2016 column detailing why I could not vote for Clinton or Trump, I wrote, "Trump is an egotistical, thin-skinned demagogue, who has tapped into the vein of what is disturbing many Americans. **However, I cannot believe that he can solve their problems**".

May 2017

One Man's Opinion

Collusion or Not?

Folks who do not support President Trump, be they politicians or journalists, see collusion with the Russian government in every bit of information about contacts between Russian officials and members of the president's camp. In public statements, former intelligence officials state they have seen no evidence of collusion. How does one see the contacts but believe that this is not proof of collusion?

Intelligence operatives have continually attempted to recruit assets among government officials and military officers of adversary nations. The CIA and KGB (now FSB) use similar tactics in recruiting. Start by befriending a potential asset, learning as much as possible about the person and placing that person in compromising situations. Perhaps a male is introduced to a female and they are intimate even though the male is married. Perhaps the operative discovers that the potential asset is a homosexual or has committed some crime in his past which would have negative effects if revealed to the public. The operative might offer the unknowing target a business opportunity which might appear illegal if made public. Once the asset realizes that he is being blackmailed, he has the choice of working with the operative or suffering the consequence of public revelation.

Members of the Trump team who are not experienced in intelligence operations were easily duped into meetings or phone calls, not realizing that they might be blackmailed in the future to help Russian interests. Even if nothing as nefarious as being blackmailed into spying in the future was a possibility, having one's heart and mind open to positive feelings about their Russian connections might cause one to lose objectivity. There is no collusion here, simply the development of relationships with dark undercurrents not seen by the naïve targets. The one member of the Trump camp who has a vast background in intelligence is retired U.S. Army Lieutenant General Michael Flynn. He had to know that he was engaging in risky behavior, but he was probably blinded by the belief that he was so close to the president that he would survive any problem. His motives might have been for financial gain or to influence U.S.-Russia relations to a point where he would become an historical figure.

The various investigations in progress will certainly find questionable contacts between Trump team members and Russian officials but it is highly doubtful if any evidence of collusion will be found. There may be penalties for errors or omissions made in completing government security forms and maybe a lie or two to the FBI, but no serious crimes. Naivety, yes, maybe even stupidity, but minimal criminality.

The journalists and politicians should allow the investigations to be completed without unneeded comments and meanwhile, get back to putting our nation on a path to success for its population.

June 2017

One Man's Opinion

President Trump's Legacy

It is not too early to start thinking of President Trump's legacy. Fifty years from now, will he be remembered like Teddy Roosevelt, as a great leader, or as Herbert Hoover, who many blame him for the Great Depression? If we examine the first year of the Trump presidency, we might be able to predict his legacy. Unless you are a liberal Democrat, you must be pleased with much of what the president has accomplished in 2017.

The economy is doing well, with GDP growth over three percent for the last two quarters. The stock markets are booming, and this benefits many. Anyone with a 401-K or an IRA has done quite well this year. For example, if you are invested in an S&P 500 index fund, your investment is worth twenty percent more than it was at the start of the year. Retail sales are doing very well, and unemployment is lower that it has been in many years.

Justice Neil Gorsuch is an excellent replacement for Justice Scalia. Although ISIS is still a dangerous terrorist organization, their caliphate is gone, following a successful military campaign abetted by the U.S. If Republicans are right, most citizens will see a financial benefit from the new tax bill. Given all these positive results, one might ask, "Why is the president's rating so low?" The percent who support President Trump has dropped to thirty-five, and this must be corrected if a proper legacy is to be expected.

Supporters claim the low ratings are due to the media which seem to delight in presenting the president in the most negative light. This is not the primary explanation. When asked about the president's performance, those who voted for the president expressed frustration with his tweets and oral statements which demeaned those who oppose him. They support his goals but wish he would take a more mature road in his communications.

Donald Trump wants to be supported and certainly seeks to leave a positive legacy. What must he do? Two simple steps would lay the foundation for a groundswell of support for the president. First, stop tweeting demeaning messages. He might recall his mother telling him that if you cannot say something nice, then say nothing at all. The second action is to bring the leaders of both parties from both houses of Congress together and demand that they seek compromise on fixing the nation's problems — immigration, infrastructure, Social Security, Medicare and cyber security. If Congressional leaders will not cooperate in the best interests of the nation, the president can go on television and call them out.

With positive presidential leadership, America can be as great as it ever was, and Donald Trump can build a legacy for the ages.

December 2017

One Man's Opinion

The Future of NATO

President Trump has made remarks indicating that NATO is "obsolete". Immediately, his political opponents chastised him for denigrating NATO. Perhaps the president should slightly amend his words to be more accurate and thus allow his comments on NATO to be more productive. The president should announce that NATO's mission has evolved and if the member nations do not address the new mission, then the organization will become obsolete.

When formed seven decades ago, the primary objectives of NATO were halting the spread of communism in Europe and being a bulwark against Soviet military aggressiveness. Few care about communism today and the Soviet Union is gone. In today's world, NATO's primary objectives should be stopping international terrorism and protecting member nations from Russian military aggression. Terrorist networks are global and only a multi-nation approach will be effective in quashing terrorist acts. NATO has the structure to infiltrate and frustrate terrorist plots but needs the leadership of the U.S. in this mission — the FBI, CIA and the New York City Police Department are at the forefront of anti-terrorist actions.

The Russians have demonstrated their aggressive behavior with the invasion and annexation of Crimea. In 1994, the U.K., U.S., and Russia signed a treaty which guaranteed the independence, sovereignty, and the existing borders of Ukraine, if Ukraine relinquished its nuclear weapons. The weapons were surrendered, yet Russia has violated the treaty it signed. Some folks believe that Russia was justified in annexing Crimea since that territory had once been part of Russia and a sizable proportion of the Crimean population speaks Russian. Anyone who agrees with this position must support a Mexican invasion and annexation of Arizona since our state once belonged to Mexico and a significant portion of Arizonans speak Spanish!

Had Ukraine been a member of NATO, would Russia have invaded? Article 5 would have dictated that a threat to Ukraine was a threat to all member nations. In a recent interview on Fox News, Tucker Carlson asked the president why his (Tucker's) son should be sent to fight in Montenegro and the president had no answer. Since Montenegro is a NATO nation, U.S. troops could be sent to defend this small country. The answer to Tucker's concern is simple. After 9/11, NATO invoked Article 5 and European troops were sent to fight in Afghanistan in support of Operation Enduring Freedom. Al Qaeda did not attack Belgium or Italy or Germany, yet these NATO members sent troops, some of whom came back home in body bags. That should answer Tucker!

President Trump seems to react best to concerns of his supporters. If you are a supporter and agree with this article, please communicate this to the White House.

A more accurate assessment of NATO's future will be a benefit to President Trump, to the U.S. and to the world.

July 2018

One Man's Opinion

Promises in Conflict

Two of the most significant promises made by candidate Donald Trump in the 2016 election were to end illegal immigration and to greatly enhance manufacturing in the U.S. These goals appear to be in conflict. On August 28, an army of ICE (Immigration and Customs Enforcement) agents swooped down on a factory in North Texas. The plant took steel plates, molded them, and welded the pieces to manufacture trailers for use in agriculture and at the oil fields. ICE put 150 of the factory's employees on buses to be processed as undocumented immigrants. These workers represented 25% of the factory's workforce. Financial consequences for the factory's owners have yet to be determined.

There are similar factories in this area, all of which are unable to find a sufficient number of workers with the proper skills who are willing to work in these trailer manufacturing workplaces, despite paying wages between $20 and $25 per hour. They hire the undocumented who are qualified and happy to work there.

The effort to catch and deport undocumented workers is limiting the productivity of these factories. Factory owners who were interviewed indicated that unless a solution was found to allow their companies to hire and keep skilled workers, they would close their operation and move their plants to Mexico, thus eliminating a few thousand jobs and reducing American manufacturing output

As with many of our nation's problems, there appears to be a simple, workable solution, if the President and Congress would put their heads together to solve the issue. What is needed is a guest worker program, to allow foreign nationals to enter the U.S. legally for a specific job for a specific period. The workers would be registered and pay taxes on their earnings. The tax records could be used to ensure that the worker does not overstay his or her visit. Severe fines could be used to punish employers who continue to use undocumented workers.

When a worker is no longer at the specified job, he or she will have a set time (perhaps six days) to report to a border office to exit the U.S, legally. A guest worker who fails to do this will be placed on a "do not hire" list and, if found to be in the U.S., will be deported without the need for a hearing.

The workers would be able to work without fear of deportation. The companies will have a legal source of needed labor and the state and federal governments can easily track these guest workers given the technology which exists today.

As a bonus, the guest workers will not spend their life savings to be guided illegally into the U.S. and will not be at the mercy of the "coyotes' who prey upon folks trying to enter our nation to work.

October 2018

One Man's Opinion

Solving Two Major Problems at Once

There are two major problems facing the U.S, that can be solved with one coordinated solution. The ever-growing national debt is not going away. In fact, the debt will be growing soon. Every year the federal government spends more than it takes in, and the Treasury borrows the money to make up the difference. The difference is the deficit and what is borrowed adds to the national debt. The U.S. Treasury sells bills, notes, and bonds that comprise the national debt. To motivate the purchase of the new debt, interest rates must be raised. This causes other interest rates to inflate mortgages, car loans, business loans, etc. It is imperative to control the national debt.

The other major problem is the apparent inability of President Trump's goals to be realized. Most Americans support improving healthcare, lowering, and simplifying taxes, building new infrastructure, controlling immigration, and enhancing the American economy, yet no legislation has been passed. The only action that has been accomplished has been done through executive orders, and an executive order can be overturned by the next president. President Trump has no experience in government, and this has reduced his effectiveness in realizing his goals.

How can one coordinated solution solve both challenges? The president should assign Vice President Pence to take on the task of getting legislation passed. He is a former member of Congress and is respected by both sides of the aisle. As a former governor, he understands how to overcome inertia in the legislature. The vice president is a loyal subordinate and as he accomplishes getting needed legislation passed, he will give full credit to President Trump.

Meanwhile, the president will return to Manhattan where he will focus on completing major real estate deals, something at which he excels. It will be known that ALL profits from these deals will be applied to lowering the national debt. The president's deal-making skills will take a bite out of the federal indebtedness.

Anyone reading this column who has contact with White House Chief of Staff General Kelly should contact him immediately and get the ball rolling before it is too late.

October 2018

One Man's Opinion

Impeachment

Among Democrats, there is much discussion of plans to impeach President Trump. Before continuing this planning, consideration should be given for unintended consequences. Impeachment was designed by our founders to eliminate from office somebody who had committed serious crimes. Yes, President Clinton committed perjury to cover up an improper relationship, and many saw his impeachment as a partisan effort to remove a president who was disliked by many Republicans. The Republican-controlled House voted for impeachment, but it requires sixty-seven senators to vote for removal from office and there were not enough Republicans in the Senate to find Clinton guilty.

Unless a legitimate smoking gun is found linking the president to a serious crime, there will not be twenty Republican senators who will vote for Trump's removal. In 1998, voters turned on Republicans because of the impeachment and Democrats prevailed in that mid-term election. Without convincing proof of a real crime, many voters will see the impeachment as a partisan effort by Democrats and will vote against Democratic candidates in 2020.

What can folks who want to remove the president do, rather than go down the impeachment path? The president is loyal to very few, among whom are Donald Jr., Eric, Ivanka, and Jared Kushner. Finding evidence of improper actions by any or all of these members of the Trump family will result in indictments leading to an acceleration in the president's frustration. This might convince him to resign the presidency or to commit some vengeful act that crosses the line, for which impeachment is appropriate.

Our nation desperately needs Congress to work in a bipartisan fashion to address serious problems which are not going away. Certainly, an impeachment process will not contribute to this needed bipartisan action. An attempt at impeachment without meaningful evidence will harm the U.S. and harm opportunities for Democratic candidates in 2020.

Surely Democratic leaders can see the counterproductive nature of advancing impeachment.

January 2019

Acknowledgments

I wish to acknowledge Zannie Carlson, my editor, whose talents allowed my thoughts to be published, and Penny Steward, who turned me from someone who hated writing to an avid writer.

About the Author

Murray Siegel grew up in Brooklyn, NY, received an engineering physics degree from NYU, and entered the USAF out of ROTC. He was a B-52 electronic warfare officer, spending weeks on alert, flying 22-hour airborne alert missions over the Arctic, and completing bombing missions over North and South Vietnam. After leaving the Air Force, he started a career in the investment business, rising quickly to an executive position with a regional bond underwriter. Realizing that making rich people richer was not his purpose, he began forty-four years of teaching mathematics at all levels, from first grade to graduate school. He received a Ph.D. in mathematics education from Georgia State University.

While living in Georgia, he had a weekly show on WRNG, Atlanta's news/talk radio station at the time. This focused his attention on news and politics. He came to believe that ignorance is not bliss; ignorance is ignorance. Whether it was stamping out mathematical ignorance in his classroom or challenging political ignorance through his writing and speaking, Murray saw bringing intelligent, rational thought to political discourse as part of his life's mission. Since he retired from teaching, he has devoted himself to writing for various periodicals. The *Maricopa Monitor* is a weekly newspaper in the town where Murray has lived since 2007, and this became his primary vehicle for expressing his political opinions in a column entitled, "One Man's Opinion".